**Edition Schott**

T0085251

**Tobias Picker**
b.1954

# Ghost Aria

from *Thérèse Raquin*
for Tenor and Piano

Libretto by Gene Scheer
Based on the novel by Emile Zola

ED 30042

**SCHOTT**

www.schott-music.com

Mainz · London · Madrid · New York · Paris · Prague · Tokyo · Toronto
© 2000 SCHOTT HELICON MUSIC CORPORATION, New York · Printed in USA

# TOBIAS PICKER

## Ghost Aria
from *Thérèse Raquin*
for Tenor and Piano

Schott Helicon Music Corporation

ED 30042

# Ghost Aria

from "Thérèse Raquin"

Gene Scheer

Tobias Picker

Touch me. Touch me. Moth - er, touch me. Touch me. Touch me. Feel me. Feel

me. Feel my em - brace._____ I____ am the_____ shad - ow____ veil -

- ing____ your face._____ Dark____ as a soul_____ that____ can____

**Schott Helicon Music Corporation**

254 West 31st Street, 15th Floor
New York, NY 10001
Tel: 212 461 6940
Fax: 212 810 4565
ny@schott-music.com

ISBN: 978-1-61780-328-4
ISMN: M-800011-27-6

ISBN-13: 978-1-61780-328-4
Distributed By
**HAL LEONARD**
49018267   9 781617 803284